Looking Back at
Clothes and Fashion

EDITORIAL PLANNING
AMR

M
MACMILLAN

First published 1988

Published by
MACMILLAN EDUCATION LTD
Houndmills, Basingstoke, Hampshire RG21 2XS
and London
Companies and representatives
throughout the world

Author: Anne Mountfield

Designed and typeset by The Pen and Ink Book Company Ltd, London

Illustrations by Jane Cheswright, Frank James, Douglas Hall, Sally Launder, Kay Dixey

Picture research by Liz Rudoff

Printed in Hong Kong

British Library Cataloguing in Publication Data

Looking back at clothes and fashion. – (Looking back at).
  1. Clothing and dress– History– Juvenile
  literature
  I. Title
  646'.3'09   GT518

  ISBN 0-333-43941-4
  ISBN 0-333-43946-5 Series

Photographic Credits

t=top b=bottom l=left r=right

The author and publishers wish to acknowledge, with thanks, the following photographic sources: title, (Victoria and Albert Museum, London); 18, 19*t*, 21*t*, 29*t*, 43, Bridgeman Art Library, London; contents, 13*b*, 21*b*, 25*t* and *b*, 29*b*, 39*t* and *b*, Mary Evans Picture Library, London; 5*l*, 26*l*, (British Museum); 34 (L.J. Anderson Collection); Werner Forman Archive, London; 5*r*, 22, 32, Michael Holford; 8, 10, 31*b*, Hutchison Photograph Library, London; 16, 17, I.C.I. Fibres Division; 4, 9*b*, 11*r*, 23*b*, Peter Newark's Western Americana; 19*b*, (photograph Matteini), Rex Features, London; 16-17, 40, Ann Ronan; 38, Scala, Italy; 35, (photograph David Leah), Science Photo Library, London; 31*t*, Victoria and Albert Museum, London; 6, 7*l* and *r*, 9*t*, 11*l*, 14, 15, 26*r*, 34-35, 36, 37, 41*l* and *r*, 42, Zefa, UK;
Cover photograph courtesy of Bridgeman Art Library and The Victoria and Albert Museum, London
The publishers have made every effort to trace the copyright holders, but if they have inadvertently overlooked any, they will be pleased to make the necessary arrangements at the first opportunity.

Note to the reader
In this book there are some words in the text which are printed in **bold** type. This shows that the word is listed in the glossary on page 46. The glossary gives a brief explanation of words which may be new to you.

Contents

Introduction

People wear clothes for many reasons. Some people live in cold places. They have to keep warm. Other people live in hot countries and have to cover up their skin, so the Sun does not burn it. In places where the weather changes all the time, people need to change the kind of clothes they wear. What people wear also depends on what they are doing.

▲ This picture of North American Indians was painted over 100 years ago. Most of their clothes are made of animal skins. The cloaks are worn with the fur inside. The outside is decorated. The Iroquois in the centre is wearing a woven blanket and woven belt.

The first clothes

When hunters wore animal skins, they found that the skins kept them warm. In cold countries, people started to wear fur clothes. They learned to sew the skins together. They used needles made from the bones of animals or fish. The thread was made from strips of skin or from the stems of plants.

In hot countries, the Sun kept people warm. The people did not need many clothes. Sometimes, they wore a kind of apron, made from the bark of trees. Sometimes, they made skirts by tying leaves or grasses together. These clothes were worn mostly for decoration. Long, loose clothes also helped to shade people's bodies from the Sun.

Perhaps, people first wore clothes as a kind of magic too. They painted their faces and made patterns on their skin. They thought this would frighten away their enemies. They also thought it would keep away evil spirits. They wore lucky charms, called **amulets**. These were made from the bones, claws and teeth of animals, sharks' teeth, or from wood or stone. People believed that spirits lived in animals, plants and rocks. Hunters killed wild animals and wore their skins. They believed that if they did this, they would be strong like the animals.

Belts and necklaces are some of the oldest forms of clothing. They were used to hang amulets around people's waists or necks. Belts could also be used for carrying hunting weapons and tools.

▲ The Indians of the plains of North America made necklaces like this. There are bear claws fixed to it. Only the bravest men were allowed to wear bear claws.

Making clothes

People learned to spin thread and to weave the thread into cloth. In some places, they used the wool from the animals they kept. In other places, they made cloth from plants, such as cotton or flax. Chinese people made cloth from a special kind of thread. It was spun by silkworms.

Cloth was easy to cut and sew. Clothes could be cut and made to fit the shape of the body. This is called **tailoring**. In hot countries, cloth was often **draped** in folds around the body. Draped clothes are cool to wear in warm weather.

▼ This statue shows how a young girl from a wealthy family dressed in Roman times, about 2000 years ago. The material of her dress is draped in folds around her body.

Keeping warm and cool

Hundreds of thousands of years ago, the northern half of the Earth was covered by ice. People could not live there. They lived in the warm, green lands of the south, in places like Africa. When they learned to make fire and to wear animal skins, they could keep warm. They began to move north.

Clothes for warmth

One way to keep warm, in the past, was to cover the body with mud. Animal skins were also warm, but they soon dried out and went stiff. At first, people tried to soften the skins by chewing them or hammering them. Then, they found that they could soften the skins by rubbing them with oils. People also softened the skins by soaking them. They used a liquid from the bark of trees. This is called **tanning**. Tanning made the skins soft enough to sew.

Cave paintings of hunters have been found which are thousands of years old. They show that the hunters wore hooded jackets. They are very much like the fur jackets that some of the Inuit people wear today. Until about 40 years ago, wearing animal furs was the only way to keep warm in the frozen lands of the north. Soldiers who went there to fight wore the same clothes as the Inuit. The army paid Inuit women to make fur clothes for them. Now, furs can be made

▲ The Inuit people live in the far north. They need very warm clothes. Some still wear fur jackets and boots, as their ancestors did. They also wear modern clothes. These men are wearing trousers made of ordinary cloth.

in factories. They look like animal furs, but they are not made from skins. These artificial furs are light to wear, and cost less to buy than real fur.

Clothes to keep cool

Long ago, people in hot countries kept cool by wearing very few clothes. Animal skins were too hot and too heavy to wear as protection from the Sun. Important people were often fanned with feathers or leaves to keep them cool.

When people learned to make cloth, they could cover themselves with light clothes. Clothes helped to keep the Sun from burning their skin. In Malaysia, men and women wrap a strip of cloth around their bodies. The loose end is tucked in at the waist, or under the arms. This strip of cloth is called a **sarong**. Near dry, sandy deserts, people wear flowing robes in the daytime. These robes allow the air to blow through them. In this way, people are kept cool. Sometimes, desert people wear a mask of cloth over their mouths. This keeps out sand and dust. At night, it is cold in the desert. People wrap themselves in blankets to keep warm. In India, some women drape a long length of cloth, called a **sari**, around their bodies.

▼ These women are from Bali, in Indonesia. Their skirts are made from long strips of cloth called sarongs. They may be made of silk or cotton. They are about four metres long, and are usually in very beautiful colours.

◄ The Tuareg people live in the Sahara Desert. The men wear turbans. They wrap the cloth around their heads and faces. This protects them from sandstorms. The clothes they wear are loose so they can stay cool in the desert heat.

Decency and decoration

People have very different ideas about what to wear. There are people who live deep in the forests of hot countries. They wear only a belt or a lip ornament. That is their way of dressing.

Decency

In parts of the Middle East, people cover up all of their bodies. They do not like people to see their bodies. The women cover their faces with veils.

▲ In some Middle Eastern countries, women keep their faces and their heads covered. This woman is a Bedouin. She is wearing a special veil over her face called a yashmak. A Bedouin woman will not let any man see her face, except her husband.

People's religion also tells them how to dress. Sikh men wear a long piece of cloth on their heads. They wind it into a **turban**. Jewish men cover their heads when they pray. Muslims leave their shoes outside a temple. They worship barefoot. Some Buddhists wear orange clothes. Some Christian women cover their heads when they go to church. Many brides, all over the world, still cover their faces with a veil on their wedding day.

Decoration

Some people like to paint their faces and make patterns on their bodies. For thousands of years, they have decorated their bodies in this way. Sometimes, the patterns were cut into the skin. The cuts were often stained with dye. Sometimes, they were made by pricking the skin with a needle. Coloured dye was put into the needle holes. These patterns are called **tattoos**. Even before they knew how to make clothes, people put flowers and feathers in their hair. They wore necklaces made from shells, seeds or bones.

People have also decorated their clothes. They painted patterns on animal skins. Sometimes, they cut the ends of the skins into strips, or fringes. Beads were sewn on to skin clothes. Cloth was woven in patterns or dyed. It was often stitched with coloured threads. A pattern made with threads is called **embroidery**.

▶ These dancers are from Papua New Guinea. They have decorated their bodies and their faces. They have used mud, paint and charcoal or ash to make different patterns.

The patterns on the cloth had circles and triangles. These were often like the patterns on body tattoos.

Trimmings were added to clothes as well. Ribbons, lace, even gold and jewels, were stitched on to the cloth. The collars and sleeves might be edged with fur. People began to sell each other fine cloth, or **fabric**, and trimmings.

Some people like to be noticed. They like wearing clothes in styles that are new. They enjoy wearing clothes that make them feel good. This is called 'being in fashion'. Early ideas of fashion started with the decoration of the body and clothes.

▲ The Indians of North America made beautiful clothes from a soft leather called buckskin. They decorated their clothes with fringes, beads and dyes. This shirt made by the Sioux people has weasel skins stitched to it. These show that the wearer was an important person.

Natural materials

People first made clothes from plants or animal skins. These are **natural materials**. They come from things that live and grow. People used whatever they could find. Some materials, like leaves, could be worn just as they were. Some, like animal skins, had to be softened to make them comfortable to wear. Other materials, like wool, had to be spun into thread. The thread was woven into cloth.

Trees, leaves and grasses

In hot, damp forests, many plants have large leaves. People tied leaves together and made skirts. Grasses were plaited into belts or made into skirts. Some people still wear clothes made in this way. In Samoa, skirts are made from leaves. In Hawaii, they are made from grass.

In Africa and South America, the inside of the bark of trees was used to make clothes. It was beaten until it was thin. Then, it was soaked and cut into strips. The strips were laid on top of each other. As they dried out, they stuck together. When the bark dried, it was soft. It made a kind of cloth.

Plants

Many plants have parts which are long and stringy. These are called **fibres**. People learned to use plant fibres to make cloth. In ancient Egypt, flax stalks were made into linen thread. The thread was then made into cloth. Aztec women, in South America, used the leaves of a cactus plant.

▼ These men are from the Solomon Islands, in the Pacific Ocean. They wear grass skirts for traditional dancing. They usually wear modern clothes. You can see that they have shorts on under their skirts.

▲ The cotton plant grows in hot countries. It is a small bush. Its seeds grow in a kind of pod called a boll. This boll is filled with white, fluffy fibres. These are used to make cotton thread.

Cotton grows in the hot, damp countries of Asia, Africa and the United States. White, silky hairs grow around the seeds of the cotton plant. Cotton thread can be made from these silky hairs.

Animals

People made clothes from the skins of the animals they hunted. The people of North America hunted buffalo, deer, beaver and fox. The Inuit people hunted caribou and seal. In Central Asia and Northern Europe, people wore the skins of sheep and goats. They used calf skins to make leather for shoes.

People learned to use the animals' hairs , too. They made them into woollen thread. Then, they made the threads into cloth. They used hair from sheep, goats, camels and llamas. Animal hairs could also be pressed together. The pressed hair made a cloth called **felt**.

In China, 5000 years ago, people knew how to make silk. Silk comes from the case, or **cocoon**, that a silkworm makes around itself before it turns into a moth. The silkworms were kept on special 'silk farms'. Silk cloth is very thin and light. It can be draped and folded. Many saris are made of silk. Silk can also be cut and made into shirts, dresses or scarves.

▼ The Plains Indians from North America hunted the buffalo. They used the skins for clothes and to make tents. The women scraped these skins clean, and tanned them and dried them out. It took six days to tan one skin.

Tools and machines

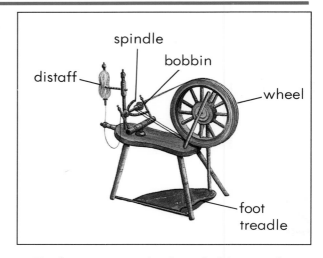

distaff
spindle
bobbin
wheel
foot treadle

▲ The first spinning wheels probably came from India. The wheel was turned by hand. In the 1700s, there was a new kind of spinning wheel. This one had a treadle. The person spinning could work the treadle with their feet to make the wheel turn.

Needles are the oldest tools used for making clothes. The first needles were made from bones or animal horn. Bone needles have been found that are 40 000 years old. Metal needles were made about 5000 years ago. We know that metal scissors were made about 2000 years ago. Needles and scissors are still used today. Their shape has not changed at all.

Spinning

One of the first tools for making thread was called a **distaff**. The distaff is a long wooden stick with a groove cut in one end. It is held under one arm. A lump of raw wool or plant fibre is pushed on to the distaff. The loose ends of the fibres are joined together and twisted around a bar of wood with a pin in it. This smaller stick was called the **spindle**. The spindle had a weight on it. This twisted around and around. As it turned, it pulled out the fibres into a long thread. This is called spinning the thread. The thread, or **yarn**, was wound around the bottom of the spindle. Many people still spin in this way.

For more than 500 years, wooden spinning wheels have often been used to turn the spindles. The yarn was spun at home by women. That is where the word 'spinster' comes from.

In 1764, a British cloth maker, called James Hargreaves, invented a spinning machine. It was called the Spinning Jenny. With this machine, one person could spin several threads at once.

Weaving

The threads were woven into cloth. The cloth was made on a wooden frame called a **loom**. Two sets of thread were needed. One set of threads, called the **warp**, was held in place by the loom. The second thread was called the **weft**. It was wound around a small pointed holder called a **shuttle**. The weavers passed the shuttle over one warp thread and under the next. As the shuttle went across, and then back, it made rows of weft threads. The weavers pushed the rows of weft threads together. This is how the cloth was made.

▲ This weaver is working on a loom. He is passing the shuttle carrying the weft thread between the warp threads.

About 200 years ago, looms were driven by water and steam power. Huge factories were built along the banks of rivers. In many countries, spinning and weaving no longer took place at home. Cloth making became quicker and easier.

Sewing machines

For thousands of years, clothes were sewn by hand. Then, about 200 years ago, sewing machines were invented. Isaac Merrit Singer, an American, first sold sewing machines in 1852. These machines had a wheel which the sewer turned. It made the needle go up and down. Sewing machines could sew hundreds of stitches in a minute. Today, factory machines sew thousands of stitches in a minute. The sewer does not turn the wheel by hand. The machines work by electricity.

▼ This type of sewing machine was used in 1905. The design did not change for a long time. There are still plenty of machines like this today. They work using a treadle. The person sewing has both hands free to hold the cloth.

13

Folk costume

What are you wearing today? What would your clothes tell the people you meet? Would they know where you come from by how you dressed? People who lived in the same place used to wear the same kind of clothes. Sometimes, other people knew which village they lived in by the style of their hats, or the colour of their skirts. Clothes which were worn by the people of the countryside are called folk costume.

Rich and poor

Rich people could wear different clothes. They could change the styles if they wished. They did not make their own cloth or their own clothes. They bought all kinds of cloth, cotton, silk and velvet. Some of this cloth came from far-away countries. The people who sold the cloth were called **merchants**. They travelled to many countries to buy the cloth. They brought back news of what other people wore. The new styles were copied.

People who lived far away from towns and cities made their own clothes. They did not hear about new styles very quickly. Their clothes stayed the same for hundreds of years. Also, poor people did not have many clothes. They took care of the clothes they had. These clothes were made of strong materials. They often lasted a lifetime. Poor people had one set of clothes to work in and one set for special occasions. These clothes were often embroidered with patterns of flowers and leaves. Sometimes, they were decorated with lace. They were passed on to other members of the family when the person who first wore them died or grew too big for them.

◀ There are many different kinds of folk costume in Europe. People from Europe took these costumes with them to North America and Australia. Today, they are only worn for special for special festivals. This costume is from the Ukraine.

▲ These Iranian women are wearing traditional clothes. They will only wear these clothes on special occasions, such as weddings. They usually wear a long black robe called a chador.

American folk costume

The American Indians had their own style of clothes. These varied from group to group. For example, the woodland Indians of the Great Lakes, wore flowered aprons. The Sioux, who lived on the plains, used patterns of triangles and crosses on their clothes. People who came to America brought their folk costumes from other countries with them.

Costumes in Asia and Africa

In many parts of the world, clothes have not changed very much at all. In India, women wear saris made of cotton or silk, or trousers and long **tunics**. In the Middle East, many men wear long robes with a cloth covering the head. In China and Japan, some people still wear dark jackets and trousers to work in. On special days, they might wear a long silk coat. In Japan, this is called a **kimono**. These coats are often embroidered. Today, western styles, like jeans and T-shirts, are worn in towns all over the world. These factory-made clothes are cheap, but they mean that colourful folk costume is not worn as much as it was.

▼ Women in India have been wearing saris for over 2000 years. They are often made of cotton printed with patterns which are only from one area.

New materials

Until about 200 years ago, most people wore cloth which was made at home, or near where they lived. It was called **homespun** cloth. Local materials, such as sheep's wool, were used to make it. Chinese silks and Indian cottons cost a lot of money. They had to be carried long distances over land and sea.

Then, machines made it quick and easy to make cloth. Trains and steamships brought fabrics from across the world. The fabrics were less expensive now. This made more and more people want to buy them. So more cloth was needed. How could it be made quickly and at a low price?

New cloth from plants

Some people try to find out more about the world. They are called scientists. In 1663, an English scientist, Robert Hooke, had the idea of spinning gum into thread. About 200 years later, this idea was tried out. Scientists used wood pulp, or **cellulose**. It is a natural material and is found in plants. The scientists turned the cellulose into a liquid and heated it. Then, they poured it through very fine holes. The liquid became hard and turned into threads.

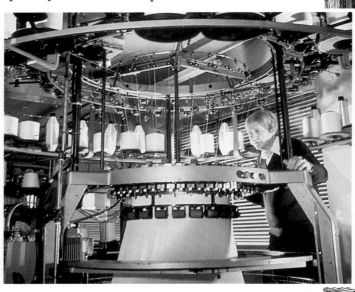

▲ Today, there are many kinds of synthetic fibres. They are made from chemical mixtures. Most synthetic fabrics are less expensive than natural fabrics. This factory in Britain is making a fabric which is used for sportswear.

Rayon

Fibres which are made by people are called **synthetics**. In 1889, a Frenchman called Hilaire de Chardonnet, made a new material. The material made by Chardonnet looked like silk. He used wood pulp and **nitric acid**, but it kept on exploding! Then, a safer way was found. People called the new thread 'rayon'. It was strong and did not cost a lot of money. Today, many fabrics have rayon in them. This is mixed with other fibres such as cotton or wool.

Nylon

Nylon was invented in the United States in the 1930s. Scientists mixed **chemicals** from coal tar and oil. Nylon was the first fibre to be made in this way. There are now many other fibres of this kind. They are strong, wash easily and keep their shape.

Synthetic materials are not expensive to make. Today, garments like shirts, sweaters and raincoats can be made out of these new materials. In the future, the world's oil may become scarce. People will have to think of new ways to make material for clothes.

▼ Skiers need to have clothes that are warm, light and strong. They need to stretch, so they stay close to the body. Today, synthetic fabrics can do all these things. They can be made in bright colours as well.

◀ These men are working in a factory in France in 1898. They are making Chardonnet silk. This was the first kind of rayon. Working in the factory could be dangerous. The chemicals they were using caught fire easily and exploded.

17

Changing fashions

What is fashion? It is a style of dressing which many people like to wear. Most fashions used to begin at the courts of kings and queens. Only rich people rushed to copy the latest styles. These clothes were very expensive. They were worn to impress other people. Often, they were decorated with jewels and gold thread.

About 200 years ago, Marie Antoinette was Queen of France. Rose Bertin made the queen's clothes. Each month, she sent fashion dolls to other courts. The dolls were dressed in the queen's latest styles. People copied these styles. Soon, the French court led the fashion in Europe and America.

Styles from other countries

In some countries, the styles in clothing have changed very slowly. Rich people in the Middle East, China and India wore finer clothes than poor people. The fabrics cost more and they were decorated with jewels. However, rich and poor people wore the same shaped clothes. The styles suited the way people lived. They stayed the same for hundreds of years.

In Europe, the styles and shapes of clothes changed faster after the 1200s. New ideas often came from travellers. They had seen different clothes in other parts of the world. During the 1100s and 1200s, knights from Europe travelled to wars in the Middle East. These wars are called the **Crusades**. The men brought back some new styles to Europe. Women in Europe began to wear veils like the women in the Middle East did.

People who make up new styles are called designers. They often copy the styles and fabrics used in other countries. Chinese silk and shawls that came from Kashmir in India have been used for a long time. They are still very popular today.

◀ Marie Antoinette was Queen of France in the late 1700s. She was famous for the amount of money she spent on clothes . The dress she is wearing in this ballet was designed and made just for her. The costumes were made of silk. They were decorated with jewels.

▲ These Japanese women are wearing kimonos. The kimono is a traditional Japanese dress. It is a bit like a dressing gown. It is worn with a piece of cloth wrapped around as a very wide sash. Only young women had kimonos with these very long sleeves.

Laws about fashion

Before 1600, there were laws in Europe about fashion. These laws were made to stop people from trying to look too important. Rich merchants and their families could not wear silks and furs. These laws stopped a hundred years later. Another law about clothes was made in Britain. It was passed to help the sale of wool. All men had to own a woollen cape. They had to wear them on Sundays.

The fashion industry

When people make, buy and sell one kind of thing, we say it is an **industry**. The fashion industry of today began in Paris. Rose Bertin is the first dress designer whose name we know. In 1858, another royal designer, Charles Worth, began selling clothes in Paris.

French designers such as Christian Dior and Coco Chanel were leaders of fashion about 30 years ago. Today, many countries have fashion industries. France, Italy, Japan and Britain lead the world in clothes design. New styles are put on show for summer and winter. Fashion shows are held in many countries. Shortly after these shows, cheaper ready-to-wear copies of the clothes can be found in local shops.

▲ Today, fashion is big business. Designers show off their ideas to buyers at fashion shows.

19

The shape of clothes

The first clothes we know about were very simple in shape. Sometimes, the cloth was not cut at all. People folded or draped it around their bodies.

Draped clothes

Cloth can be draped to make a cape, a skirt or a scarf. Saris are a kind of dress made by draping. A strip of cloth, five to six metres long, is folded and draped around the body.

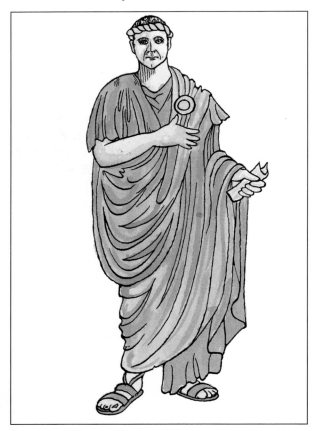

▲ Roman togas were often so long that they were awkward to wear.

About two thousand years ago, Roman men wore loose garments called **togas**. A toga was made from woollen cloth. It was folded around the body and the right arm was left free. Togas became very large. Some measured seven metres across.

Tailored clothes

Clothes which have been cut into shapes are called tailored clothes. The first tailored clothes were simple. In Central and South America, people cut a hole in the middle of a piece of cloth. They put it on over their heads. It hung down over the shoulders. The garments are called **ponchos**. They are often made of wool and are very warm. All over the world, simple tunics were made by joining two pieces of cloth at the shoulders and at the sides. The tunics could be belted around the waist. Sleeves, hoods and collars were later added if they were needed.

Changing shape

In some places, the shape of clothes has changed very slowly. In China and Japan, women and men wore loose, long-sleeved gowns. These gowns had no collars. They were belted at the waist. The basic shape remained the same for thousands of years. In other countries, many new shapes and styles have developed.

▶ This painting shows an archery contest in China in the 1700s. The government officials are all wearing the same kind of clothes. These are silk robes with square panels on the front and back. The style of the panel showed how important the wearer was.

In Europe, about 600 years ago, men and women often wore two tunics. The tunic worn under the outer tunic was longer. In time, women's longer under-tunics became skirts and dresses. The short tunics on top became blouses and jackets. About 500 years ago, men's top tunics were called **doublets**. This was because they were made from double layers of cloth with padding in between. Up to 100 years ago, men and women still wore cloaks out of doors.

For hundreds of years, men wore short trousers called **breeches** and long, cloth stockings called **hose**. In the 1800s, men began to wear suits with long trousers and fitted jackets. They wore cloaks or overcoats over them.

▶ In the 1850s huge stiffened underskirts called crinolines were the fashion. The artist who drew this thought crinolines were a silly fashion. They were never really this big.

Unusual clothes

In Europe, people have worn some very strangely shaped clothes. In the 1600s, people wore huge frilled collars called **ruffs**. In the Netherlands, some ruffs were like cartwheels. Two hundred years later, women's skirts were held out by stiffened frames called **crinolines**. These were like large lampshades and they made it very difficult for women to sit down!

Trousers and skirts

In Central Asia and the USSR, trousers have been worn for a long time by both men and women. In the Greek and Roman Empires, only farmers and slaves wore trousers. In hot countries, men first wore skirts draped around their waists. Today, many women all over the world wear trousers, but not many men still wear skirts.

Skirts

In ancient Egypt, men and women wore only one garment. This was a skirt. Later, women wore tunics. The tunics became longer and looked more like dresses. Men's skirts grew longer, too. They were divided in the middle. They became loose cotton trousers. In Fiji, Malaysia and Scotland, men still wear skirts. The Scottish national dress for men is a pleated skirt called a **kilt**.

In many Asian countries, like India and Sri Lanka, men still wear cloth wrapped around their waists. The Indian **dhoti** is a length of cloth made of light cotton. It can be worn loosely like a skirt. For work, the back part is usually pulled through the legs and tucked into the waist. This makes loose trousers.

Trousers

Roman soldiers first saw trousers when they went to war in Northern Europe. The people who lived in what is now Germany, France and Britain wore them. The Romans did not copy the style. They thought that only wild, fierce people wore trousers.

▼ This papyrus from ancient Egypt shows us that the men wore just a short skirt. This was made by wrapping a cloth around the waist. Some of the men have fastened this cloth with a belt.

dhoti

short breeches late 1500s

French 1600s

late 1800s

In Europe, over 500 years ago, men who worked on the land wore loose, baggy trousers. Land-owners wore trousers that fitted tightly around the leg. This showed that the land-owner did not have to work on the land. About 100 years later, knee-length trousers were worn.

Trousers for women

In Asian countries, women have always worn trousers. In Europe, women did not wear them until about 100 years ago. The idea of women wearing trousers was shocking. In 1851, an American woman called Amelia Bloomer shocked people by wearing baggy trousers under a short skirt. These 'bloomers' caused a great fuss.

Very few women dared to wear trousers in public until the 1940s. Then, during the Second World War, women had to work in factories and on the land. Trousers were much easier to work in than a skirt. Since that time, more and more women have worn trousers.

▲ These drawings show how trousers have changed. At first men wore a cloth around the waist. Then to make moving around easier, they tied a piece of cloth between their legs.

▲ Amelia Bloomer owned a newspaper in America in the 1800s. At that time, women's clothes were hard to move about in. She used her newspaper to encourage people to allow women to wear 'bloomers'.

Underwear and nightwear

Underwear was first worn to keep the outer clothes clean. It also stopped the garment from scratching the skin. Until about 500 years ago, few people had special clothes to sleep in. Most people slept in their underwear, or without any clothes at all.

Women's underwear

Some clothes need underwear to keep them in place. Indian women wear ankle-length underskirts. Their short-sleeved tops are called **cholis**. The sari is wrapped around the underskirt and tucked into it. The long end of the sari is draped over one shoulder of the choli.

Roman women wore sleeveless tunics under their clothes. For many years, these tunics, called **shifts**, were the only underwear women wore throughout Europe. Then, they began to wear underskirts, called **petticoats**, for extra warmth. Roman women also wore a kind of bra. This idea was not copied. The type we know today was first worn only about 70 years ago.

About 300 years ago, French women wore long silk trousers. They were called **drawers** and were worn under their skirts. The style was copied from the ones worn in Asia. People thought it was wrong for women to wear trousers, even hidden ones. Most women in Europe did not wear short **knickers** until about 80 years ago.

Men's underwear

Men who lived in cold countries were the first to wear undergarments. Over 800 years ago, men in Europe wore undershirts and short, baggy drawers. In the 1800s, men often wore woollen undershirts or vests. They had ankle-length underpants called 'long johns'. Today, most men wear short underpants and sleeveless vests.

Changing shapes

Underwear can be used to change the shape of the body. Over 300 years ago, women wore hidden rolls of cloth stuffed with wool. These **farthingales** made their skirts stick out at the hips. In Europe, about 150 years ago, men with skinny legs wore padding to make it appear they had large leg muscles. Later, women's skirts were held out by crinoline hoops, or padded at the back with **bustles**.

▼ Fashions in underwear have changed over the years, for men and women.

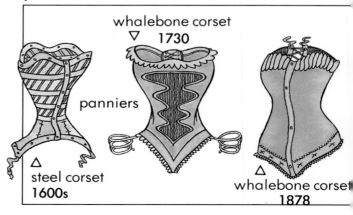

steel corset
1600s

whalebone corset
▽ 1730

panniers

whalebone corset
1878

Nightwear

About 400 years ago, most people in Europe wore night clothes. Men wore plain shirts and women wore shifts. Both men and women wore nightcaps in bed to keep their heads warm. Three hundred years later, men began to wear jackets and trousers in bed. This fashion was copied from garments worn during the day in India. The new outfits were called pyjamas.

▲ This cartoon was drawn in 1820. At the time, women used corsets or stays to make their waists very small. It was a very uncomfortable fashion. There was never a machine like this. The artist is just showing how silly the fashion was.

▼ This is the style of nightdress worn in the 1900s. It was made of soft warm fabric, and it was very loose. It was much more comfortable than day-time clothes.

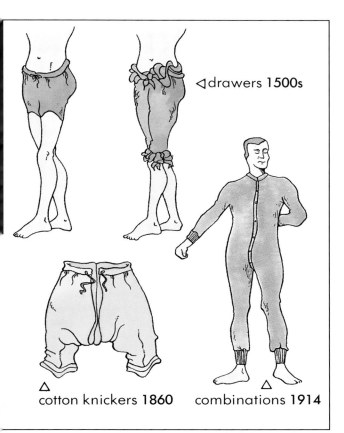

◁ drawers 1500s

△ cotton knickers 1860

△ combinations 1914

Jewellery and cosmetics

We know that long ago, people wore jewels and gold for decoration. Gold and precious stones do not decay. Necklaces and rings look just like they did when they were first worn. Many of these things have been found in tombs, or buried under the ground. Jewels were often worn as charms. Roman boys wore gold necklaces called **bullas** for luck. In Sicily today, some children still wear a kind of bulla. It holds a red coral bead.

In many countries, men and women wore gold and jewels to show that they were rich. Kings and queens wore crowns made from gold and precious stones. At weddings, gifts of jewellery were often given to the bride.

Today, jewellery is often not made with real stones. It is made of paste which looks like jewels. It is called costume jewellery.

▲ Gold has been used for jewellery for thousands of years. This head-dress was made about 5000 years ago for a queen. It comes from the Middle East. It is made of gold and a stone called lapis lazuli.

▲ This woman is from Pakistan where it is the custom to wear a lot of beautiful jewellery. She is even wearing jewellery in her hair and a jewelled nose pin.

Make-up

For hundreds of years, people have painted their faces. Sometimes, they did this to scare off their enemies. The ancient Britons painted their bodies with blue dye. They made the dye from a plant called **woad**. North American Indians made up their faces before they went to fight. Many other people did this, too.

In ancient Egypt and Asia, people painted their faces, too. They thought it made them look beautiful. They drew dark lines around their eyes with a paint called **kohl**. Egyptian women used orange colour on their lips and cheeks. They painted their fingers and toe nails with a coloured varnish. In Egypt, Japan, and later in Europe, women rubbed their faces with white lead. This was very dangerous. Lead is a poison and it eats into the skin.

Face paints and oil for the skin are called cosmetics. The Roman poet, Ovid, wrote a book about healthy cosmetics. He told people to mix eggs, bean flour and flower roots with honey. The mixture made a paste. It was spread on the face to make the skin softer.

About 300 years ago, men and women in Europe wore a great deal of make-up. Men often wore more make-up than women. The noblemen in France painted their eyes and cheeks, and wore face powder. They grew their finger nails long. This was to show they did not have to work with their hands. Chinese rulers also grew very long nails.

▲ In the past both men and women wore make-up. They often reddened their lips and cheeks. Sometimes they made their faces white and plucked their eyebrows to make their faces more like a mask.

About 100 years ago, make-up had gone out of fashion in Europe. Women in Europe and America did not dare to paint their faces or nails. The most girls could do was to bite their lips to make them red! Few women used much make-up until the 1940s. Now, women use as much, or as little, make-up as they want. Men are beginning to wear it again, too. In Europe and North America, many young men make up their faces. The young pop stars of the music world have led this fashion.

Hats, hairstyles and wigs

People used to think the head was very important. Rulers wore crowns or head-dresses on their heads. They wore them to show that they were important people.

People also needed to protect their heads from the cold or from the hot Sun. They wore hats to do this. In battles, they wore helmets to keep their heads safe from injury.

Hats

The first hats were often made from animals skins or feathers. In Africa and North America, bird feathers were worn. The North American Indians thought feathers carried prayers to heaven. Between 100 and 200 years ago, it was a fashion in Europe to wear ostrich feathers on hats. Women wore these feathers fixed into their hair in the evening.

In cold countries like Tibet or the USSR, hats often have ear flaps. In hot, wet countries like China and Malaysia, straw hats with wide brims keep the Sun and the rain off the head. Sometimes, hats were worn for other reasons. In Greece and Rome, skull caps meant that you were not a slave. You were a free person.

Veils

Many women covered their heads with a veil. In Asia, the veil often covered the face as well. In Europe, women often covered their hair and their chins, but they did not veil their faces. In the 1400s, it was the fashion for women to wear tall pointed hats. Veils were sewn on to the points. These hats were called **hennins**. For about another 200 years, both men and women wore hats indoors. Then, in Europe, it became usual for men to take off their hats indoors.

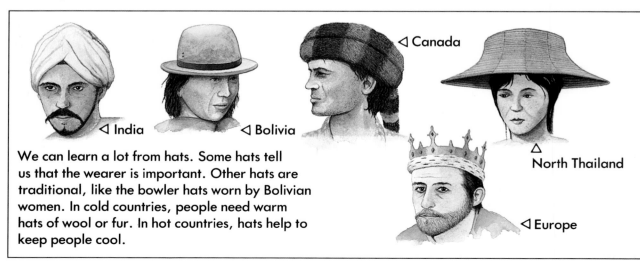

◁ Canada

◁ India

◁ Bolivia

△ North Thailand

◁ Europe

We can learn a lot from hats. Some hats tell us that the wearer is important. Other hats are traditional, like the bowler hats worn by Bolivian women. In cold countries, people need warm hats of wool or fur. In hot countries, hats help to keep people cool.

Hairstyles and false hair

Hairstyles have also been changed by fashion. About 3500 years ago, in the Near East, Assyrian men sometimes wore false beards. In Greece and Rome, men wore their hair short. There were barbers' shops in Roman towns. Women often curled and frizzed their hair. The Romans also used **bleach** to dye their hair blonde.

In the 1600s, men in Europe used to shave their heads. They wore false hair called wigs. Long curled wigs were made from animal hair. Later, the wigs were tied back in plaits or pigtails, with bows. Women also wore wigs. Sometimes, they built their own hair up on metal frames to look like a wig. These head-dresses often held feathers, model ships or baskets of fruit! Both men and women put white powder on their hair. In England, the government made money out of this style. Every time any hair powder was sold, some money had to be sent to the government. So powder cost more and more money. Hairstyles soon became plainer!

▲ The fashion in the 1400s was to wear a tall tight-fitting cap or hennin. This woman has covered her head with a stiffened veil. No hair was supposed to show, so she shaved her hairline back.

◁ Holland

France 1600s ▷

▲ During the 1780s, the fashion was to have a lot of hair. This was curled, powdered and decorated with bows and lace. Women also wore hats and bonnets with a lot of trimming.

29

Top to toe

Shoes, gloves and umbrellas are all parts of clothing. They protect our feet, our hands and our heads from the heat, the cold and the rain.

Sandals and shoes

Sandals were the first footwear. They were made by cutting a piece of leaf, skin or wood to the same size as the foot. This made the sole of the sandal. It was tied to the foot, or held on by a toe string.

Simple shoes were made by wrapping leather around the foot. The leather was held with a criss-cross lace. Roman women wore woollen foot coverings under their shoes. They were called *soccus*. The word has now become 'sock'. North American Indians wore soft leather shoes called **moccasins**. In some countries, shoes were carved from a piece of wood. These wooden shoes, called **clogs**, were strong and heavy. People also wore wooden overshoes to keep their feet dry. The shoes were called **pattens**. They were wooden soles which were strapped over other shoes. When people wore them, they could walk through mud and water. Their feet stayed dry.

▶ The Romans and Greeks wore sandals. These protected the soles of the feet. They kept the feet cool. In cold countries, people needed to keep their feet warm and dry. They wore shoes. Some shoes were made just to look good. They were made of embroidered silk or soft kid leather.

Fashions in shoes changed too. Sometimes, toes were pointed, or square. In the 1400s, men wore shoes with long pointed toes. The points were so long that they were fastened to the knees! It was not until about 400 years later that left and right shoes were made. Before that, they were straight. They could be worn on either foot.

Greek sandals

pointed boots 1400s

◁ man's shoe 1600s

Moroccan slipper

lady's boot late 1800s

Japanese shoes

◄ We wear gloves for all sorts of reasons. Some gloves keep our hands warm. Other gloves keep them clean or dry. These gloves are not meant to do any of those things. They are fashionable gloves worn for decoration. Some of the gloves have no fingers. They were worn indoors.

Umbrellas

The word umbrella means a 'shade maker'. The first umbrellas were used in China over 3000 years ago. They were held to shade the Chinese rulers from the sun. For a long time, umbrellas, or **parasols**, were used only as sunshades. Then, in 1750, a British man began a new fashion. He held an umbrella up to keep the rain off his head!

Gloves

People tied cloth or fur around their hands to keep them warm. This was the first kind of glove. These **mittens** covered all the fingers together. They were difficult to work in. In Asia, gloves were unknown. There, sleeves were made with long cuffs to fold down in cold weather. In other countries, sewn or knitted gloves with fingers were used. Sometimes, the ends of the fingers were left uncovered to make work easier. Gloves were often embroidered, or trimmed with lace and jewels.

Longer gloves covered the wrists and arms as well as the hands. These were called **gauntlets**. Leather gauntlets were worn by people who used hunting birds. The birds perched on their wrists. Metal gauntlets were a part of suits of **armour**. They were worn in battle.

▼ This government official is from Chad, in West Africa. The decorated umbrella carried beside him shows that he is an important man.

Buttons and bows

Fur and skin clothes were first held together by thorns, or by long, sharp bones. Then, when people began to use metal, they made pins. The pin was pushed in and out of the cloth. Then, a **clasp** at the back of the pin held it safely shut. Pins were decorated. They were bent into shapes, or made to hold coloured stones. These pins are called brooches.

▲ People have used buckles for fastening belts and waistbands for centuries. This buckle is over 1000 years old. It was made by Anglo-Saxon people in Britain. It is solid gold and weighs nearly half a kilogram. It is very skilfully decorated with a snake design.

The Greeks and Romans used pins and brooches to fasten their draped clothes. The Celtic peoples of Northern Europe pinned their cloaks at the shoulder with fine brooches. They were round and were often made from gold. Sometimes, they were decorated with jewels and **enamel**.

Buttons

In the northern parts of Britain, skeletons have been found with rows of buttons down their fronts. The buttons are carved from animal bone. They may be all that remains of clothes that were worn 5000 years ago. Buttons do not seem to have been used in many places until about 700 years ago.

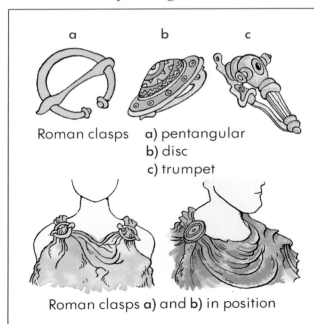

Roman clasps a) pentangular
b) disc
c) trumpet

Roman clasps a) and b) in position

Between 600 and 700 years ago, clothes were more tightly fitted. Buttons began to be used to fasten gowns and sleeves. They were also sewn on to clothes for decoration. By the 1700s, buttons were often made from silver and precious stones. They were sewn on coats to show that people were rich. Later, long rows of buttons were used, not just on clothes, but on boots and gloves. Special **button hooks** were sold to help fasten them.

Ribbons and bows

Clothes can also be fastened by tying the ends of a piece of cloth together. This makes a knot. North American Indian clothes were often tied together with laces made from thin strips of animal skin. In hot countries, simple clothes were tied together with plaited grass.

▼ Buttons and bows have been used to fasten clothes for thousands of years.

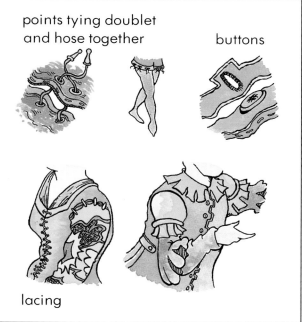

points tying doublet and hose together

buttons

lacing

Over 400 years ago, clothes in Europe were often tied with lengths of ribbon, called **points**. Sometimes, the points were tied in a bow. They decorated a sleeve or a trouser leg. Since then, bows have often been used to decorate clothes. Shoe laces and apron strings are still tied together with bows.

Zip fasteners

About 300 to 400 years ago, clothes began to be fastened with metal hooks and eyes. Hooking them took a long time. In the 1890s, an American, called Whitcomb Judson, invented a way to lock metal hooks and eyes together quickly. He used these early zips to fasten special shoes to be worn in the rain. The Hook and Eye company of New Jersey, in the United States, sold them as 'C-Curity'. They did not sell well because they did not always stay together!

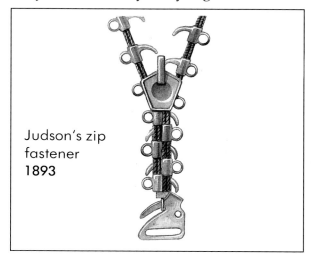

Judson's zip fastener 1893

▲ Hooks and eyes have been used to fasten clothes sinces the 1500s. At the end of the 1800s, the first zip fastener was invented. Today, we often use zip fasteners, and they are now mostly made of plastic.

Protective clothing

Some jobs need special kinds of clothes. They may be worn to keep people safe, or clean.

Protection in battle

Soldiers need special clothes to protect them. Greek soldiers' tunics were made of leather and metal. Their helmets were trimmed with coloured horsehair. Over 700 years ago, special tunics were worn. These were made by linking small rings of metal together. This was called **chain-mail**. Two hundred years later, armour was made from flat plates of metal. These were tied together.

Today, soldiers need light clothes that are bullet-proof. They also wear clothes which make them hard to see. The clothes are green and brown and black. This is called **camouflage**.

Waterproof clothes

We do not like to wear wet clothes. People learned how to keep water out of their clothes. They rubbed them with linseed oil. Oilskins were used for hundreds of years. Sailors found oilskin very useful at sea. Sailors are sometimes called 'Jack Tars'. This is because their clothes used to be made from **canvas**. The canvas had been covered with tar.

◀ These suits of armour are from Japan. They date from the 1700s. They are made of iron and wood, and then painted with lacquer.

◀ Modern fire-fighting clothes work very well, These people can stand quite close to a gas explosion.

Keeping clean

Until about 200 years ago, many people did not know that dirt spread diseases. Patients died because hospitals were dirty. Today, when operations are done, everyone wears clean clothes. The nurses and doctors wear long gowns and they cover their mouths with masks. They wear thin rubber gloves and often use paper caps and masks. These are used once and then thrown away.

People who make and sell food also need to keep clean. They must cover their hair while they work. In many factories, the workers wear special caps, gloves and overalls. These clothes protect the workers. They also keep their work clean. People who work in places where medicine is made must be extra careful.

About 200 years ago, Charles Macintosh, a Scottish chemist, made cloth coats which were lined with rubber. People called them Macintoshes after him. They kept out the rain. So we say they are waterproof. We also call them raincoats.

Heatproof clothes

People who work in hot places like furnaces need to keep cool. People who fight fires need to be protected. In 1879, **asbestos** cloth was first made. This could protect people against heat. Today, special suits are made. They have a metal in the fabric. It is called **aluminium**. These suits do not burn. They are fire-proof. Some suits have special pipes in them. The pipes are used for breathing. Firemen can wear these suits right inside a fire. They will still be safe.

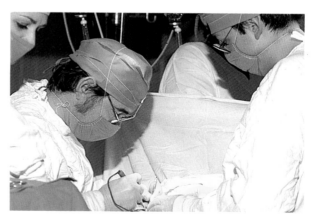

▲ Doctors wear protective clothing in operating rooms. Before the doctors wear them, the garments are treated to kill all the germs.

Special clothes

Clothes can tell us a lot about people. They can tell us what job they do. Sometimes, clothes tell us how important a person is.

Rulers and priests often wear special clothes and colours. Maori chiefs in New Zealand wore cloaks made of feathers. These were not needed to keep them warm. They were worn as a sign of power. In Africa, chiefs wore leopard skins. North American Indian chiefs wore eagle feathers. The eagle is one of the largest and fiercest of birds. The braver the chief, the more feathers he wore. Important Romans were allowed to wear togas with purple edges. No one but the Emperor could wear a toga that was dyed purple all over.

Today, kings and queens wear crowns and robes on special days. Leaders of towns or cities in Europe wear cloaks and special necklaces or brooches. On special days, Christian bishops wear tall hats called **mitres**. Sometimes priests' clothes are very simple. Buddhist monks shave their heads and wear orange robes. Christian monks and nuns dress in dark-coloured clothes. These people dress alike to show that they belong to a group.

▶ These are Buddhist monks from Tibet. The monks are wearing robes for a ceremony. There are several groups of Buddhist monks in Tibet. These belong to a group called the Yellow Hat sect.

Uniforms

Sometimes groups of people wear special clothes. They dress alike. They are wearing a uniform. Uniform means 'the same'. Soldiers first wore uniforms to show which side they were on. Sports players often wear uniforms for the same reason. The players, and the people watching them can see each side easily. Police officers wear uniforms too. So do nurses in hospitals. They wear uniforms so they can be seen easily if needed.

Uniforms show what jobs people do. They need to be smart and practical. They also need to be comfortable and easy to keep clean.

Weddings and funerals

People wear special clothes for weddings and funerals. In many European countries and in North America, brides often wear long white dresses at weddings. In Japan too, women may wear white kimonos when they get married. In some parts of India, brides wear red saris.

In China, white is worn as a sign of sadness. White clothes are worn at funerals. In many other countries, people wear black when someone dies.

▶ Weddings are always a time for wearing special clothes. This is a Hindu wedding in Madras. A Hindu bride often wears a red sari. This bride has a golden sari. She carries a special flame. The wedding is carried out in front of this flame.

37

Clothes for free time

When people are not at work, they like to relax. Some people play sports. Other people go on long walks, or sail boats. Many people like to work in their gardens, or sit and rest. They wear clothes that are comfortable and easy to wash.

Special clothes for sports have been worn for a long time. In Sicily, there is a picture that is 2000 years old. It shows a Roman girl in a sports hall. She is wearing a bikini and holding weights. She can move around easily.

Sports clothes have not always been easy to move around in. In the 1880s, women played tennis in long skirts and hats! At the beginning of the 1900s, women wanted to ride bicycles. Their long skirts caught in the wheels. So they began to wear divided skirts, or baggy knee-length trousers called **knickerbockers**.

▼ Bikinis are nothing new. This picture comes from a Roman villa. We can see that Roman women wore bikinis to do gymnastics.

▶ Today, women wear comfortable sports clothes, just as men do. It was not always like that. This is a tennis game in 1880. Women had to play in long skirts and tight jackets. Over the years, women began wearing shorter and looser clothes.

Sports clothes are also worn to protect the body. American footballers wear huge, padded clothes and helmets. Jockeys who ride race-horses, wear hard hats. They also wear bright silk shirts. These help people to see who is winning the race.

Clothes and the seaside

Over 100 years ago, swimming in the sea became a fashion. Doctors said it was very healthy. People were very shy about swimming. They did not want to undress in public. They were carried to the edge of the water in wagons. Then, they stepped into the water behind a screen. They wore their underclothes for swimming.

Later, seaside holidays became popular. Women's 'bathing suits' had knee-length skirts. Men's bathing suits had long legs and sleeves. In the 1930s, sun-bathing became a new craze. Swim-suits no longer covered the arms and legs, but they were still one piece. The two-piece swim-suit, or bikini, came into fashion in the 1950s.

Evening dress

Sometimes, when people go out in the evening they like to wear special clothes. Women often wear long dresses and jewels. They want to look elegant. Men often wear dinner jackets and bow ties. They may even wear long 'tailcoats'. This style of dressing is called 'evening dress' and is worn at special times.

▲ This advertisement for bicycles was printed in 1895. The young woman is wearing knickerbockers. It was the latest fashion for cycling. It was a very daring fashion to wear, when most women kept their legs covered right down to their ankles.

Making and selling clothes

Long ago, rich people could buy silks and furs from other lands. Weavers sold rough homespun cloth at markets and fairs. Sometimes, people took the cloth home to sew. Sometimes, they paid a tailor or a dressmaker to sew for them. Hats, gloves and shoes are difficult to make. They were sold in shops or on market stalls by the people who made them.

Pins, ribbons and buckles were sold by travellers called **pedlars**. Pedlars did not make these goods. They bought them cheaply from other traders. They displayed them on their pushcarts at markets. They also took their goods from door to door.

By the early 1800s, many people in Europe had moved from the country to work in towns. The poorest people who lived in towns hardly ever bought new clothes. Instead, their clothes came from second-hand clothes stalls, or **rag fairs**. Other people in towns did not have time to make their own clothes. They bought their clothes from a tailor or a dressmaker.

In the shops, customers were shown dressed dolls, or coloured pictures of the latest fashions. When they had chosen the style they liked, the dressmaker made it in their size. Until the mid-1850s, dressmakers had to make their own paper patterns and had to do all the sewing by hand.

◀ In the past, all clothes were made by hand. In the 1800s, things began to change. This picture shows hatters, milliners and tailors in 1871. Most are working by hand. Some are already using machines.

Clothing factories

In 1830, a French tailor, Barthélemy Thimmonier, set up a factory in Paris. He had 80 sewing machines. He wanted to make clothes for the French army. People thought the factory would take work away from hand-workers. His machines were smashed. In the United States, sewing machines changed the old ways. They meant that clothes could be made in factories. Instead of buying a fabric and choosing a pattern, people could buy clothes ready-made.

People were paid very low wages for making clothes. The factories were often dark and unhealthy places. There was not much room for the workers. Sometimes, people were given machines to use at home. They were paid 'by the piece' for each garment. They had to work long hours to make enough money to live on.

These factories, or **sweatshops**, were often the only places where people could find work. In 1890, a news reporter visited the East Side of New York. He said the streets were filled with 'the whirr of a thousand sewing machines, working from dawn until mind and muscle gave out together'.

▼ In a modern clothes factory, there are machines to do much of the work. This machine can cut out many garments at once. In the past, dressmakers cut clothes out one by one. This machine makes the job faster and clothes less expensive.

▲ This is a modern dressmaking factory. The workers use sewing machines. They are modern machines. Unlike the old sweatshops, this factory is light and clean. The jobs people have to do are still much the same.

Children's clothes

Clothes for young children were first made over 200 years ago. Before that time, children were usually dressed in baby clothes until they were three or four years old. Then, they were dressed in the same styles as their parents.

Baby clothes

In many countries, babies were often wrapped tightly in cloth. Strips of cloth bound their arms and legs to their sides. People thought that babies needed these clothes to make their bones grow straight. Babies wore this cloth for about nine months. In some parts of Eastern Europe, and among some North American Indians, these **swaddling clothes** are still used.

Then, over 100 years ago, babies began to wear long dresses and shawls in North America and Europe. Boys stayed in dresses until they were about four years old.

Special children's clothes

In the 1800s, boys often wore sailor suits or knee-length trousers. They also wore a cap. A boy's first pair of trousers made him feel very grown-up. Young girls wore **smocks** over their dresses. They also wore dresses with long **pantalettes** underneath. Older girls wore ankle-length skirts. They could wear their hair pinned up. It was a sign that they were old enough to marry.

▲ This little girl is wearing traditional Japanese clothes. Children in Japan do not usually dress like this, but they used to. It must have been very hard to play in these long clothes.

▶ These are the Clark children. This picture of them was painted in 1840. The youngest is a boy, but he is wearing a dress. The little girl is still wearing quite a short skirt. Her older sister and brother are already in grown-up clothes.

Rich people's children were dressed in embroidered silks. Their clothes had lacy collars and jewels as decoration. It cannot have been very easy to play in these clothes.

Most children did not have clothes like that. They wore simple clothes, made by a relative or a friend. They wore clothes that they could play and work in. Poor children began work when they were about five years old. In some places, they still do.

Fashions for young people

Fashions for young people are quite a new idea. In the 1950s, young people had more money to spend than ever before. They began to develop fashions of their own. In the late 1950s, in Britain, many young men wore long jackets, tight trousers and greased their hair back. They were called 'Teddy Boys', because they wore the fashions of the days of King Edward VII.

Young people's fashions are often meant to shock. Young men's shoulder-length hair shocked people in the 1960s. Girls' mini-skirts, which were very short, shocked people in the 1960s and 1970s. Spikey, brightly coloured hair, or no hair at all, shocked people in the 1970s and 1980s. Often these 'shocking' fashions are like fashions which have been worn in the past.

▼ New fashions happen all the time. Some are more popular than others. Some of the oddest clothes are for young people. When the fashion has gone past, people start to think the clothes look very strange.

Quiz

How much can you remember about this book? Try this quiz and use the glossary and index to help you check your answers.

1. Here are the names of four famous dress designers with the letters mixed up. Try to find the correct names. **Clue**: They all worked in Paris.
    a) TOWRH,   b) RIDO,
    c) NERITB, d) HAECNL

2. Match the descriptions given in (a) to (f) with the words numbered (1) to (6) below them.

    a) A skirt held out by hoops
    b) A dark eye paint
    c) A South American cape, put on over the head
    d) A woman's underskirt
    e) A bishop's hat
    f) A head covering worn by men in India

    1) poncho
    2) turban
    3) crinoline
    4) kohl
    5) petticoat
    6) mitre

3. Complete the following sentences with (a), (b), (c) or (d):

    1) A method of softening animal skins by soaking them in a liquid is called
    a) tattooing   c) tailoring
    b) tanning   d) draping

    2) One of the first tools for making thread was called a
    a) spindle   c) spinster
    b) hennin   d) distaff

    3) In Asia, some women cover their faces with
    a) parasols   c) veils
    b) wigs   d) togas

    4) Gauntlets cover:
    a) the legs and feet
    b) the nose and ears
    c) the wrist and arm
    d) the heel and toes

    5) Farthingales were rolls of padding worn under:
    a) jackets   c) shoes
    b) skirts   d) hats

4. Which is the odd one out? Why?

    a) breeches, bloomers, doublet, drawers
    b) sari, toga, jacket, sarong
    c) wig, sandal, crown, helmet
    d) silk, wool, nylon, cotton
    e) petticoat, cloak, corset, shift

5. Are these statements true or false?

    a) Rayon is a natural material
    b) Felt comes from the bark of a tree
    c) Weaving is done on a loom
    d) Buttons were not used until the 1800s
    e) Pattens were wooden overshoes, on an iron ring

6. Who

    a) shocked people in 1851, by wearing trousers?
    b) gave his name to raincoats?

c) sold the first sewing machines for home use?

d) invented the first zip-fasteners?

7. What

a) machine did James Hargreaves invent?

b) thread was invented in the United States in 1937?

c) colour is used as a sign of sadness in China?

d) is the name for a charm which protects against evil?

8. Why

a) were sailors called Jack Tars?

b) did Roman boys wear bullas?

c) were babies dressed in swaddling clothes?

d) do some Arab women wear veils?

9. Each of these sentences names a piece of clothing. The name has had the letters mixed up. Try to find the correct word.

a) Soldiers wore METHESL on their heads to protect them.

b) MONOIKS are loose robes, worn in Japan.

c) The IKIBIN is a two piece swim-suit.

d) North American Indians wore CSNISOCAM made from soft leather on their feet.

e) Women in India wear a short-sleeved top called a HLCOI under their sari.

10. Which part of the body is covered by:

a) a clog? b) a mitten? c) hose d) a shawl? e) a hennin?

Answers

1. (a) Worth (b) Dior (c) Bertin (d) Chanel

2. (a) 3, (b) 4, (c) 1, (d) 5, (e) 6, (f) 2

3. (1) b, (2) c, (3) c, (4) c, (5) b

4. a) doublet (all the others are types of trousers)
b) jacket (all the others are draped clothes)
c) sandal (all the others are worn on the head)
d) nylon (all the others are natural materials)
e) cloak (all the others are types of underwear)

5. (a) False, (b) False, (c) True, (d) False, (e) True

6. (a) Amelia Bloomer, (b) Charles Macintosh,

7. (a) the Spinning Jenny, (b) nylon, (c) Isaac Singer, (d) Whitcomb Judson

8. a) because their clothes were painted with tar to make them waterproof b) to keep away evil spirits and to bring them good luck c) because people believed that it would make their arms and legs grow straight d) so that no man, except their husband, can see their face

9. (a) helmets, (b) kimonos, (c) bikini, (d) moccasins, (e) choli

10. (a) the foot, (b) the hand, (c) the legs, (d) the shoulders, (e) the head

Glossary

aluminium: a metal which is very light. It can be made very thin to make heatproof material

amulet: something worn as a charm to protect against evil

armour: clothing or a covering of wood or metal worn as a protection against weapons.

asbestos: a mineral found in the ground. It is made up of fibres. Asbestos can be woven to make a cloth that does not burn

bleach: a liquid that takes the colour out of other substances.

breeches: trousers which come to just below the knee

bulla: a round metal ornament worn on a chain by Roman children. Bullas were also used to seal documents

bustle: the padding worn inside a woman's skirt at the bottom of her back. A bustle gave extra fullness and shape to the skirt

button hook: a small hand held tool with a hook on the end. The hook was used to pull buttons through the button holes

camouflage: the colour, pattern or body shape which helps to hide an object in its surroundings

canvas: a strong, heavy cloth usually made of cotton. It is used for making tents and sails

cellulose: a substance that plants are made of

chain-mail: a type of armour. It is made from connected links of metal.

chemical: any substance which can change when joined or mixed with another substance

choli: a round necked blouse with short sleeves which ends at the waist. It is worn under a sari by women in India

clasp: the fastening on a necklace or a brooch. The clasp attaches the brooch to the clothing

clog: a shoe carved out of a piece of wood or with a wooden bottom or sole

cocoon: the silken case which protects the pupa of a moth and other insects

crinoline: an underskirt with different sized hoops attached to it. The skirt that is worn over it stands away from the legs in a bell shape

Crusades: a series of wars when Christians fought against the Turks in the Holy Land. These wars were between the years 1000 and 1400

dhoti: a piece of cotton material worn like a skirt by Hindu men in India

distaff: the wooden stick that holds wood for spinning. The fibres of wood are then pulled from it to be spun into threads

doublet: a tightly-fitting piece of clothing for the top of the body. It was short and worn with or without sleeves

drape: a way of hanging cloth in loose folds over an object

drawers: loose underpants. Drawers are like baggy trousers

embroidery: designs and patterns usually stitched on cloth.

enamel: a glossy substance that has been joined on to metal by heating and melting

fabric: a cloth made by weaving or knitting

farthingale: a padded wheel-shaped hoop sometimes made of whalebone. This was worn around the waist and made skirts stick out at the sides

felt: a kind of thick cloth made by pressing hair or wool flat

fibre: a hair-like or thread-like part of something. Cloth is made of fibres

gauntlet: a glove with a large cuff which protects the hand, wrist and lower arm. A gauntlet was often covered with armour

hennin: a tall, usually pointed, woman's hat with a piece of thin material hanging from its top

homespun: a simple cloth or material made in the home and not in a factory

hose: tight-fitting coverings or stockings for the legs or feet. Hose was usually made of fine material like silk or wool

industry: the work to do with the making or producing of goods, often in a factory

kilt: a short pleated skirt. The kilt worn by men in Scotland is usually made of checked cloth

kimono: a long, loose robe with wide sleeves. It is usually held in place by a wide sash

knickerbockers: loose, short trousers which are gathered in at the knee

knickers: short underpants for women

kohl: a fine black powder used for darkening the eyelids. It is widely used in India, Pakistan and the Middle East

loom: a machine for weaving thread into cloth

merchant: a person who buys and sells goods. A merchant often deals with other countries

mitre: a tall head-dress which is split into two peaks at the top. A mitre is worn by bishops

mitten: a kind of glove which covers the whole hand. It does not have separate covers for each finger

moccasin: a shoe made out of pieces of deerskin or other soft leather stitched together. Moccasins were originally worn by North American Indians

natural materials: materials made from animals or things which live and grow in the world around us

nitric acid: a strong, burning liquid made by mixing different chemicals. It is poisonous and dangerous

pantalettes: long, loose underpants with a frill at the bottom of each leg. They come below the bottom of the dress

parasol: an umbrella used to give protection and shade from the Sun. Parasols are usually small and light

patten: a thick wooden sole often mounted on an iron ring. A patten can be fastened to a shoe to raise it out of the mud

pedlar: a person who goes from place to place carrying things for sale

petticoat: an underskirt which fastens around the waist. It is worn under skirts and dresses

point: a thin piece of cloth, lace or cord. It is used for fastening clothes or for tying two pieces of material together

poncho: a blanket or piece of material with a hole made for the head. The poncho hangs over the shoulders like a cloak

rag fair: a market which sells old clothes

ruff: a frill worn around the neck. Ruffs are usually made of stiffened material gathered into even folds

sari: a long piece of material worn as the main garment by Hindu women. It is folded around the body with one end over the shoulder

sarong: a long cloth wrapped around the waist like a skirt or tucked under the armpits. A sarong is worn in Malaysia by men and women

shift: a loose, shapeless dress

shuttle: a small boat-shaped tool used in weaving

smock: a loose, shirtlike garment which covers other clothing. Smocks are now usually worn by children

spindle: a rod which has two thin ends. A spindle is used to twist and wind fibres to make thread

swaddling clothes: strips of cloth which are tied tightly around a baby to stop it moving

sweatshop: a factory or shop where people have to work in bad conditions for very long hours for very low wages

synthetic: describes a material produced by combining chemicals.

tailoring: making clothes to fit exactly

tanning: a way of changing animal skins into soft leather by soaking them in a liquid. The liquid is made from oak bark or other vegetable mixtures

tattoo: a picture or pattern permanently marked on the skin. Tattooing is done by pricking the skin with needles dipped in coloured inks

toga: a piece of woollen material worn by the Romans. A toga hung loosely and covered the whole body except for the head and right arm

trimmings: additions to clothing which decorate it

tunic: a garment which hangs straight from the shoulders to the upper half of the legs. It usually has no sleeves

turban: a head-covering made by winding a long length of cloth around a cap or the head

warp: the threads stretched from the top to the bottom of a loom in weaving

weft: the threads which run across and through the warp threads in weaving

woad: a substance from a plant of the same name. Woad colours and stains things blue

yarn: a thread made by twisting fibres

Index